Born in 1994

by

kerry Butters.

Born in 1994.

Millennium:	2nd millennium
Centuries:	19th century – **20th century** – 21st century
Decades:	1960s 1970s 1980s – **1990s** – 2000s 2010s 2020s
Years:	1991 1992 1993 – **1994** – 1995 1996 1997

1994 (MCMXCIV) was a common year starting on Saturday (dominical letter B) of the Gregorian calendar, the 1994th year of the Common Era (CE) and *Anno Domini* (AD) designations, the 994th year of the 2nd millennium, the 94th year of the 20th century, and the 5th year of the 1990s decade. The year **1994** was designated as the "International Year of the Family" and the "International Year of Sport and the Olympic Ideal" by the United Nations.

Contents

Events

January

- January 1
  - The North American Free Trade Agreement (NAFTA) is established.
  - The Zapatista Army of National Liberation begins their war in Chiapas, Mexico.
- January 6 – In Detroit, Nancy Kerrigan is clubbed on the right leg by an assailant, under orders from figure skating rival Tonya Harding's ex-husband.
- January 8 – *Soyuz TM-18*: Valeri Polyakov begins his 437.7 day orbit, eventually setting the world record for days spent in orbit.
- January 11
  - The Irish government announces the end of a 15-year broadcasting ban on the Provisional Irish Republican Army and its political arm Sinn Féin.
  - The *Superhighway Summit* is held at UCLA's Royce Hall. It is the first conference to discuss the growing information superhighway and is presided over by U.S. Vice President Al Gore.
- January 14 – U.S. President Bill Clinton and Russian President Boris Yeltsin sign the Kremlin accords, which stop the preprogrammed aiming of nuclear missiles toward each country's targets, and also provide for the dismantling of the nuclear arsenal in Ukraine.

- January 15 – The SS *American Star* breaks tow in the Atlantic Ocean and is beached at Fuerteventura in the Canary Islands a few days later.
- January 17 – The 6.5–6.7 Mw Northridge earthquake shakes the Greater Los Angeles Area with a maximum Mercalli intensity of IX (*Violent*), leaving 57 people dead and more than 8,700 injured.
- January 19 – Record cold temperatures hit the eastern United States. The coldest temperature ever measured in Indiana state history, −36 °F (−38 °C), is recorded in New Whiteland, Indiana.
- January 20 – In South Carolina, Shannon Faulkner becomes the first female cadet to attend The Citadel, but soon drops out.
- January 21 – Lorena Bobbitt is found not guilty by reason of insanity on charges of mutilating her husband John.
- January 25 – U.S. President Bill Clinton delivers his first State of the Union address, calling for health care reform, a ban on assault weapons, and welfare reform.
- January 26 – A man fires 2 blank shots at Charles, Prince of Wales in Sydney, Australia.

February

William Perry

- February 1
  - In Portland, Oregon, Tonya Harding's ex-husband Jeff Gillooly pleads guilty for his role in attacking figure skater Nancy Kerrigan. He accepts a plea bargain, admitting to racketeering charges in exchange for testimony against Harding.

- o Punk rock band Green Day releases their album *Dookie*, which will eventually sell over 20 million copies worldwide.
- February 3
  - o William J. Perry is sworn in as the United States Secretary of Defense.
  - o In the aftermath of the Chadian–Libyan conflict, the International Court of Justice rules that the Aouzou Strip belongs to the Republic of Chad.
- February 4 – The Federal Open Market Committee raises the Fed Funds target rate for the first time since May 1989. The rate is raised by 25 basis points to 3¼ percent.
- February 5 – Byron De La Beckwith is convicted of the 1963 murder of civil rights leader Medgar Evers.
- February 6 – Markale massacres: A Bosnian Serb Army mortar shell kills 68 civilians and wounds about 200 in a Sarajevo marketplace.
- February 9 – The Vance–Owen Peace plan for Bosnia and Herzegovina is announced.
- February 12
  - o Edvard Munch's painting "The Scream" is stolen in Oslo (it is recovered on May 7).
  - o The 1994 Winter Olympics begin in Lillehammer.
- February 19 – Three gunmen hijack a school bus with 74 children and 8 teachers in Peshawar, Pakistan.
- February 22 – Aldrich Ames and his wife are charged with spying for the Soviet Union by the United States Department of Justice. Ames is later convicted and sentenced to life imprisonment; his wife receives 5 years in prison.
- February 24 – In Gloucester, local police begin excavations at 25 Cromwell Street, the home of Fred West, a suspect in multiple murders. On February 28, he and his wife are arrested.
- February 25 – Israeli Kahanist Baruch Goldstein opens fire inside the Cave of the Patriarchs in the West Bank; he kills 29 Muslims before worshippers beat him to death.
- February 27 – Australian Federal Sports & Environment Minister Ros Kelly resigns over "The Sports Rorts Affair", where she

allegedly apportioned money for community sporting projects in a pork barreling fashion.

- February 28 – 4 United States F-16s shoot down 4 Serbian J-21s over Bosnia and Herzegovina for violation of the Operation Deny Flight and its no-fly zone.

March

Mary Ellen Withrow

- March - unknown - The People's Republic of China gets its first connection to the Internet.
- March 1
  - A lone terrorist kills Ari Halberstam during an attack on 14 Jewish students on the Brooklyn Bridge in New York City.
  - South Africa cedes Walvis Bay to Namibia.
  - Mary Ellen Withrow begins her term of office as Treasurer of the United States, serving under President Bill Clinton.
- March 6 – A referendum in Moldova results in the electorate voting against possible reunification with Romania.
- March 7 – *Campbell v. Acuff-Rose Music, Inc.*: The Supreme Court of the United States rules that parodies of an original work are generally covered by the doctrine of fair use.
- March 12
  - A photo by Marmaduke Wetherell, previously touted as "proof" of the Loch Ness Monster, is confirmed to be a hoax.
  - The Church of England ordains its first female priests.

- March 14 – Apple Computer, Inc. releases the first Macintosh computers to use the new PowerPC Microprocessors. This is considered to be a major leap in personal computer, as well as Macintosh history.
- March 15 – U.S. troops are withdrawn from Somalia.
- March 16 – In Portland, Oregon, Tonya Harding pleads guilty to conspiracy to hinder prosecution for trying to cover-up an attack on figure skating rival Nancy Kerrigan. She is fined $100,000 and banned from the sport.
- March 20 – Italian journalist Ilaria Alpi and TV cameraman Miran Hrovatin are assassinated in Somalia.
- March 21 – The 66th Academy Awards, hosted by Whoopi Goldberg, are held at the Dorothy Chandler Pavilion in Los Angeles. Steven Spielberg's Holocaust drama, *Schindler's List*, wins 7 Oscars including Best Picture and Best Director (Spielberg).
- March 23 – Green Ramp disaster: Two military aircraft collide over Pope Air Force Base, North Carolina causing 24 fatalities.
- March 27
    - TV tycoon Silvio Berlusconi's right-wing coalition wins the Italian general election.
    - The biggest tornado outbreak in 1994 occurs in the southeastern United States; 1 tornado kills 22 people at the Goshen United Methodist Church in Piedmont, Alabama.
- March 28 – Shell House massacre: Inkatha Freedom Party and ANC supporters battle in central Johannesburg South Africa.
- March 31 – The journal *Nature* reports the finding in Ethiopia of the first complete *Australopithecus afarensis* skull (see Human evolution).

April

- April 2 – The National Convention of New Sudan of the SPLA/M opens in Chukudum.
- April 6 – Rwandan President Juvénal Habyarimana and Burundi President Cyprien Ntaryamira die when a missile shoots down

their jet near Kigali, Rwanda. This is taken as a pretext to begin the Rwandan Genocide.

- April 7
    - The Rwandan Genocide begins in Kigali, Rwanda.
    - Federal Express Flight 705 experiences an attempted suicidal hijacking. The crew manages to subdue the attacker and land at the airport.
- April 8
    - Michelangelo's *Universal Judgement* is reopened to the public after 10 years of restorations.
    - Kurt Cobain, songwriter and frontman for the band Nirvana, is found dead at his Lake Washington home, apparently of a single self-inflicted gunshot wound.
- April 16 – Voters in Finland decide to join the European Union in a referendum.
- April 19 – A Los Angeles jury awards $3.8 million to Rodney King for violation of his civil rights.
- April 20 – Paul Touvier is found guilty of ordering the execution of 7 Jews when he served in the Vichy France Milice.
    - The People's Republic of China joins the Internet.
- April 21 – The Red Cross estimates that hundreds of thousands of Tutsi have been killed in Rwanda.
- April 22 – Richard Nixon dies in New York City, nearly 20 years after he resigned in 1974. His funeral is the first funeral of a U.S. President since the death of Lyndon B. Johnson in 1973.
- April 25
    - Sultan Azlan Muhibbudin Shah ibni Almarhum Sultan Yusuff Izzudin Shah Ghafarullahu-lahu ends his term as the 9th Yang di-Pertuan Agong of Malaysia.
    - The largest high school arson ever in the United States is started at Burnsville High School, in Burnsville, Minnesota, resulting in over 15 million dollars in damages. The same arsonist also goes on to set arsons at Edina High School and Minnetonka High School.

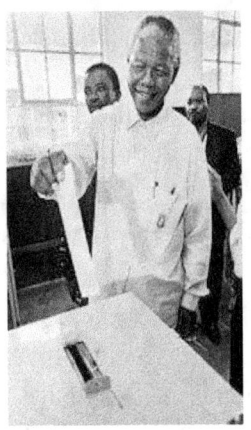

Nelson Mandela casts his vote in the South African general election, 1994

- April 26
  - Tuanku Jaafar ibni Almarhum Tuanku Abdul Rahman, Yang di-Pertuan Besar of Negeri Sembilan, becomes the 10th Yang di-Pertuan Agong of Malaysia.
  - China Airlines Flight 140, an Airbus A300, crashes while landing at Nagoya, Japan, killing 264 people.
- April 27 – South Africa holds its first fully multiracial elections, marking the final end of apartheid. Nelson Mandela wins the elections and is sworn in as the first democratic president.
- April 29 – Commodore International declares bankruptcy.

May

- May 1 – Three-time Formula One world champion Ayrton Senna is killed in an accident during the San Marino Grand Prix in Imola, Italy.
- May 5 – The Bishkek Protocol between Armenia and Azerbaijan is signed in Bishkek, Kyrgyzstan; effectively freezing the Nagorno-Karabakh conflict.
- May 6 – The Channel Tunnel, which took 15,000 workers over 7 years to complete, opens between England and France, enabling passengers to travel between the 2 countries in 35 minutes.
- May 10

- o Nelson Mandela is inaugurated as South Africa's first black president.
- o Illinois executes serial killer John Wayne Gacy by lethal injection for the murder of 33 young men and boys between 1972 and 1978.
- o An annular eclipse of the Sun is visible across much of North America.
- May 12 – Ice hockey becomes Canada's official winter sport.
- May 17 – Malawi holds its first multiparty elections.
- May 20 – After a funeral in Cluny Parish Church, Edinburgh attended by 900 people and after which 3,000 people lined the streets, John Smith is buried in a private family funeral on the island of Iona, at the sacred burial ground of Reilig Odhráin, which contains the graves of several Scottish kings as well as monarchs of Ireland, Norway and France.
- May 21 – Italian former minister and Christian Democrat leader Giulio Andreotti is accused of Mafia allegiance by the court of Palermo.
- May 22 – Pope John Paul II issues the Apostolic Letter *Ordinatio Sacerdotalis* from the Vatican, expounding the Catholic Church's position requiring "the reservation of priestly ordination to men alone".

June

- June 1 – The Republic of South Africa rejoins the British Commonwealth after the first democratic election. South Africa left the British Commonwealth in 1961.
- June 6–June 8 – Ceasefire negotiations for the Yugoslav War begin in Geneva; they agree to a 1-month cessation of hostilities (which does not last more than a few days).
- June 12 – Nicole Brown Simpson and Ronald Lyle Goldman are murdered outside the Simpson home in Los Angeles. O. J. Simpson is later acquitted of the killings, but is held liable in a civil suit.

- June 14 – Hacker Kevin Poulsen pleads guilty to 7 counts of mail fraud, wire and computer fraud, money laundering, and obstruction of justice.
- June 14 – The New York Rangers win the Stanley Cup, in 7 games over the Vancouver Canucks. It was New York's first Stanley Cup since 1940. Riots erupt in Vancouver in response to the victory causing $1.1 million Canadian dollars in damage.
- June 15
  - Israel and the Vatican establish full diplomatic relations.
  - *The Lion King*, the highest grossing hand-drawn animated feature, is released by Walt Disney Pictures.
- June 17
  - NFL star O. J. Simpson and his friend Al Cowlings flee from police in his white Ford Bronco. The low-speed chase ends at Simpson's Brentwood, Los Angeles mansion, where he surrenders.
  - The 1994 FIFA World Cup starts in the United States.
- June 20 – Dean Mellberg, an ex-U.S. Air Force member, enters the hospital at Fairchild Air Force Base, Washington, shoots and kills 5 people, and wounds 19.
- June 23 – The International Olympic Committee celebrates its first centennial.
- June 24 – U.S. Air Force pilot Bud Holland crashes a B-52 at Fairchild Air Force Base, as a result of pilot error. It's unclear whether the event of 4 days previous (above) was a contributing factor.
- June 25 - Cold War: The last Russian troops leave Germany.
- June 26 – Microsoft announces it will no longer sell or support the MS-DOS operating system separately from Microsoft Windows. This had been its mainstay since 1980.
- June 28 – Members of the Aum Shinrikyo cult execute the first sarin gas attack at Matsumoto, Japan, killing 8 and injuring 200.
- June 30 – An Airbus A330 crashes during a test flight near Toulouse, France, where Airbus is based, killing the 7-person crew. The test was meant to simulate an engine failure at low speed with maximum angle of climb.

July

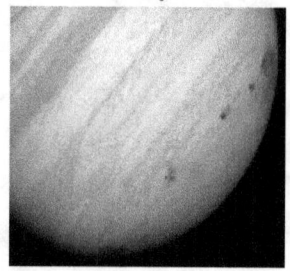

Brown spots mark impact sites of the Shoemaker-Levy Comet on Jupiter's southern hemisphere.

- July 2 – Colombian footballer Andrés Escobar, 27, is shot dead in Medellín. His murder is commonly attributed as retaliation for the own goal Escobar scored in the 1994 FIFA World Cup against the United States soccer team.
- July 4 – Rwandan Patriotic Front troops capture Kigali, a major breakthrough in the Rwandan Civil War.
- July 6 – Fourteen firefighters die in the South Canyon wildfire on Storm King Mountain in Colorado. The event inspires the 1999 book *Fire on the Mountain*.
- July 7 – 1994 civil war in Yemen: Aden is occupied by troops from North Yemen.
- July 12 – The Allied occupation of Berlin ends with a casing of the colors ceremony attended by U.S. President Bill Clinton.
- July 16–July 21 – The planet Jupiter is hit by 21 large fragments of Comet Comet Shoemaker–Levy 9 over the course of 6 days.
- July 17 – Brazil wins the 1994 FIFA World Cup, defeating Italy by 3–2 in penalties (full-time 0–0).
- July 18
    - In Buenos Aires, a terrorist attack destroys a building housing several Jewish organizations, killing 85 and injuring many more (see AMIA Bombing).
    - Rwandan Patriotic Front troops capture Gisenyi, forcing the interim government into Zaire and ending the Rwandan Genocide.

- July 19 – Four 26-pound ceiling tiles fall from the roof of the Kingdome in Seattle, just hours before a scheduled Seattle Mariners game.
- July 20 – Comet Shoemaker–Levy 9's Fragment Q1 hits Jupiter.
- July 25 – Israel and Jordan sign the Israel-Jordan Treaty of Peace, which formally ends the state of war that has existed between the nations since 1948.

August

- August 1
  - Fire destroys the Norwich Central Library in the United Kingdom, including most of its historical records.
  - The University of London founds the School of Advanced Study, a group of postgraduate research institutes.
- August 5 – Groups of protesters spread from Havana, Cuba's Castillo de la Punta ("Point Castle"), creating the first protests against Fidel Castro's government since 1959.
- August 12
  - The 1994–95 Major League Baseball strike is called, ending the 1994 MLB Season.
  - Woodstock '94 begins in Saugerties, New York. It is the 25-year anniversary of Woodstock in 1969.
- August 18 – Irish mobster Martin Cahill is assassinated in Dublin.
- August 20 – In Honolulu, Hawaii, during a circus international performance, an elephant named Tyke crushes her trainer Allen Campbell to death before hundreds of horrified spectators, at the Neal Blaisdell Arena.
- August 23 – Eugene Bullard is posthumously commissioned as a Second Lieutenant in the United States Air Force, 33 years after his death, and 77 years to the day after his rejection for U.S. military service in 1917.
- August 31
  - The Provisional Irish Republican Army announces a "complete cessation of military operations".
  - The Russian army leaves Estonia and Latvia, ending the last traces of Eastern Europe's Soviet occupation.

September

- September 3 – Cold War: Russia and the People's Republic of China agree to de-target their nuclear weapons against each other.
- September 4 – Kansai International Airport in Osaka, Japan opens. All international services are transferred from Itami to Kansai.
- September 5 – New South Wales State MP for Cabramatta John Newman is shot outside his home, in Australia's first political assassination since 1977.
- September 8 – USAir Flight 427, a Boeing 737 with 132 people on board, crashes on approach to Pittsburgh International Airport; there are no survivors.
- September 10 – *Wollemia nobilis* (the 'Wollemi Pine'), previously known only from fossils, is discovered living in remote rainforest gorges in the Wollemi National Park of New South Wales by canyoner David Noble, 150 km from Australia's largest city.
- September 13 – President Bill Clinton signs the Federal Assault Weapons Ban, which bans the manufacture of new firearms with certain features for a period of 10 years.
- September 16
  - Danish tour guide Louise Jensen is abducted, raped and murdered by 3 British soldiers in Cyprus.
  - Britain lifts the broadcasting ban imposed on Sinn Féin and paramilitary groups from Northern Ireland.
- September 17 – Heather Whitestone becomes the first hearing impaired contestant to win the Miss America entitlement. Whitestone becomes Miss America 1995.
- September 19 – American troops stage a bloodless invasion of Haiti in order to restore the legitimate elected leader, Jean-Bertrand Aristide, to power.
- September 28 – The car ferry MS *Estonia* sinks in the Baltic Sea, killing 852 people.
- September 28 – José Francisco Ruiz Massieu, Mexican politician, is assassinated on orders of Raúl Salinas de Gortari.
- September–October – Iraq disarmament crisis: Iraq threatens to stop cooperating with UNSCOM inspectors and begins to once

again deploy troops near its border with Kuwait. In response, the U.S. begins to deploy troops to Kuwait.

- Adobe Photoshop 3.0 graphics editing software released.

October

- October 1
    - In Slovakia, populist leader Vladimír Mečiar wins the general election.
    - Palau gains independence from the United Nations Trusteeship Council
- October 4 – In Switzerland, 23 members of the Order of the Solar Temple cult are found dead, a day after 25 of their fellow cultists are similarly discovered in Morin-Heights, Quebec.
- October 5 – UNESCO inaugurates World Teachers' Day to celebrate and commemorate the signing of the Recommendation Concerning the Status of Teachers on October 5, 1966.
- October 8 – Iraq disarmament crisis: The President of the United Nations Security Council says that Iraq must withdraw its troops from the Kuwait border, and immediately cooperate with weapons inspectors.
- October 12 – NASA loses radio contact with the Magellan spacecraft as the probe descends into the thick atmosphere of Venus (the spacecraft presumably burned up in the atmosphere either October 13 or October 14).
- October 15
    - After 3 years of U.S. exile, Haiti's president Aristide returns to his country.
    - Iraq disarmament crisis: Following threats by the U.N. Security Council and the U.S., Iraq withdraws troops from its border with Kuwait.
- October 29 – Francisco Martin Duran fires over two dozen shots at the White House; he is later convicted of trying to assassinate President Bill Clinton.
- October 31
    - American Eagle Flight 4184 ATR 72 crashes in Roselawn, Indiana, after circling in icy weather, killing 64 passengers.

- The Duke of Edinburgh attends a ceremony in Israel, where his late mother, Princess Alice of Battenberg (Princess Andrew of Greece), is honoured as "Righteous Among the Nations" for sheltering Jewish families from the Nazis in Athens, during World War II.

November

- November 3
  - A French magazine publishes photo of President François Mitterrand's secret daughter.
  - The Criminal Justice and Public Order Act 1994 is enacted in the UK. The whole of Part V, which covers collective trespass and nuisance on land, includes sections against raves, including the "succession of repetitive beats" definition.
- November 4
  - San Francisco: The first conference devoted entirely to the subject of the commercial potential of the World Wide Web opens. Featured speakers include Marc Andreessen of Netscape, Mark Graham of Pandora Systems, and Ken McCarthy of E-Media.
  - Sydney's third runway opens, ensuring protests about noise levels.
- November 5
  - A letter by former U.S. President Ronald Reagan, announcing that he has Alzheimer's disease, is released.
  - George Foreman wins the WBA and IBF World Heavyweight Championships by KO'ing Michael Moorer becoming the oldest heavyweight champion in history.
  - Johan Heyns, an influential Afrikaner theologian and critic of apartheid, is assassinated.
- November 6 – A flood in Piedmont, Italy, kills dozens of people.
- November 7 – WXYC, the student radio station of the University of North Carolina at Chapel Hill, provides the world's first internet radio broadcast.

- November 8 – Georgia Representative Newt Gingrich leads the United States Republican Party in taking control of both the House of Representatives and the Senate in midterm congressional elections, the first time in 40 years the Republicans secure control of both houses of Congress. George W. Bush is elected Governor of Texas.
- November 13
  - Voters in Sweden decide to join the European Union in a referendum.
  - The first passengers travel through the Channel Tunnel.
  - Michael Schumacher wins his first Formula One World Championship in controversial circumstances at the Australian Grand Prix.
- November 16 – A Federal judge issues a temporary restraining order, prohibiting the State of California from implementing Proposition 187, that would have denied most public services to illegal aliens.
- November 19 – Malawi recognizes the Sahrawi Arab Democratic Republic (SADR).
- November 20 – The Angolan government and UNITA rebels sign the Lusaka Protocol.
- November 28
  - Voters in Norway decide not to join the European Union in a referendum.
  - The Milwaukee Cannibal Jeffrey Dahmer is beaten to death by a fellow inmate at the prison where he was incarcerated.
- November 30 – The National Football League announces that the Jacksonville Jaguars will become the league's 30th franchise.

December

- December 1 – Ernesto Zedillo takes office as President of Mexico.
- December 2 – The Australian government agrees to pay reparations to indigenous Australians who were displaced during the nuclear tests at Maralinga in the 1950s and 1960s.
- December 11
  - Russian president Boris Yeltsin orders troops into Chechnya.

- A small bomb explodes on Philippine Airlines Flight 434, killing a Japanese businessman. The bombing was a field test done by Ramzi Yousef to test explosives that would have been used in Project Bojinka.
- December 13
  - The trial of former President Mengistu begins in Ethiopia.
  - Fred West, 53, a builder living in Gloucester, is remanded in custody, charged with murdering 12 people (including two of his own daughters) whose bodies are mostly found buried at his house in Cromwell Street. His wife Rose West, 41, is charged with 10 murders. Police believe that the murders took place between 1967 and 1987, and suspect that they may have killed up to 30 people.
- December 14
  - A Learjet piloted by Richard Anderson and Brad Sexton misses an elementary school and crashes into an apartment complex in Fresno, California, killing both pilots and injuring several apartment residents.
  - A runaway Santa Fe freight train rear ends a Union Pacific train at the bottom of Cajon Pass, California.
  - British Home Secretary Michael Howard announces that Myra Hindley will serve a whole life tariff for the Moors murders of the 1960s.
  - Construction commences on the Three Gorges Dam, at Sandouping, China.
- December 15 – The first version of web browser Netscape Navigator is released.
- December 19
  - A planned exchange rate correction of the Mexican peso to the US dollar, becomes a massive financial meltdown in Mexico, unleashing the 'Tequila' effect on global financial markets. This prompts a US$50 billion "bailout" by the Clinton Administration.
  - The Whitewater scandal investigation begins in Washington, D.C.
  - Civil unions between homosexuals are legalized in Sweden.

- December 26 – French anti-terrorist police storm a hijacked jet at Marseille and kill 4 Islamist terrorists.
- December 31 is skipped by the Phoenix Islands to switch from the UTC−11 time zone to UTC+13, and by the Line Islands to switch from UTC−10 to UTC+14. The latter becomes the earliest time zone in the world, one full day ahead of Hawaii.

Date unknown

- Tropical Storm Alberto and Hurricane Gordon cause very damaging floods, intense winds and extensive problems directly over the Southeastern United States and the Caribbean islands. The death tolls are unusually severe and damages are extreme in both tropical storms.
- Pyroclastic flows – clouds of scalding gas, pumice, and ash – rapidly descend an erupting Mount Merapi volcano in central Java, causing sixty deaths.
- Online service America Online offers gateway to World Wide Web for the first time. This marked the beginning of easy accessibility of the Web to the average American.
- The population of Nigeria exceeds 100 million making the republic the first African nation to have a population above 100 million.

Births

January–March

Justin Bieber

Harry Styles

Dakota Fanning

Hou Yifan

Dakota Blue Richards

- January 11 – Mathieu Marquet, Mauritian swimmer
- January 13 – Yuma Nakayama, Japanese actor and singer
- January 14 – Kai, South Korean singer
- January 18 – Gong Minji, South Korean idol singer, rapper and dancer
- January 23 – Kwak Min-jeong, South Korean figure skater
- January 29 – Ayane Sakura, Japanese voice actress
- February 1 – Harry Styles, English singer and member of One Direction
- February 5 – Saki Nakajima, Japanese singer
- February 8 – Nikki Yanofsky, Canadian singer
- February 14
  - Allie Grant, American actress
  - Paul Butcher, American actor
- February 23 – Dakota Fanning, American actress
- February 25 – Eugenie Bouchard, Canadian tennis player
- February 27 – Hou Yifan, Chinese chess player
- March 1 – Justin Bieber, Canadian pop/R&B singer
- March 5 – Aislinn Paul, Canadian actress
- March 8 – Dylan Tombides, Australian footballer (d. 2014)
- March 7 – Christina Gao, American figure skater
- March 12 – Christina Grimmie, American singer (d. 2016)
- March 13 – Gerard Deulofeu, Spanish footballer
- March 26 – Mayu Watanabe, Japanese singer
- March 29 – Sulli, South Korean singer
- March 30 – Haruka Shimazaki, Japanese singer

April–June

Aly Raisman

- April 4 – Risako Sugaya, Japanese singer
- April 11 – Dakota Blue Richards, English actress
- April 12
    - Oh Sehun, South Korean singer
    - Saoirse Ronan, Irish actress
    - Airi Suzuki, Japanese singer
- April 14 – Skyler Samuels, American actress
- April 18 – Moisés Arias, American actor
- May 4 – Alexander Gould, American actor and voice artist
- May 25
    - Aly Raisman, American gymnast
    - Kylee, Japanese-American singer
- May 21 – Tom Daley, British diver
- May 28 – Son Yeon-jae South Korean rhythmic gymnast
- June 11
    - Ivana Baquero, Spanish actress
    - Jessica Fox, French-born Australian canoeist
- June 15 – Rina Hidaka, Japanese voice actress
- June 21 – Chisato Okai, Japanese singer

July–September

Jessica Fox

- July 6 – Camilla and Rebecca Rosso, English twin actresses
- July 9 – Akiane Kramarik, American poet and artistic prodigy
- July 16 – Mark Indelicato, American actor
- August 4 – Mayuko Fukuda, Japanese actress
- August 17 – Tasuku Hatanaka, Japanese actor and voice actor
    - Taissa Farmiga, American actress
- September 1
    - Bianca Ryan, American singer
    - Jasmine, American singer
- September 12 - Mhairi Black, Scottish politician
- September 27 – Cindy Bruna, French model

October–December

- October 9 – Jodelle Ferland, Canadian actress
- October 10 – Bae Suzy, South Korean singer and actress
- October 24 – Krystal Jung, South Korean singer
- October 30 – Miyū Tsuzurahara, Japanese voice actress and child actress
- November 7 – Haruna Iikubo, Japanese singer
- November 8 – Lauren Alaina, American singer
- November 17 – Raquel Castro, American actress and singer
- November 30 – Nyjah Huston, American skateboarder
- December 3 – Jake T. Austin, American actor
- December 5 – Frida Aasen, Norwegian model
- December 7 – Yuzuru Hanyu, Japanese figure skater

- December 8 – Raheem Sterling, Jamaican-born English football player
- December 10 – Matti Klinga, Finnish football player
- December 13 – Leo Ieiri, Japanese singer
- December 16 – Stephen Sutton, English blogger and charity activist (d. 2014)
- December 29 – Princess Kako of Akishino, Japanese Princess and daughter of Prince Akishino and Princess Akishino

Deaths

January

Cesar Romero

Telly Savalas

- January 1
    - Arthur Espie Porritt, New Zealand politician and athlete (b. 1900)

- o Cesar Romero, Cuban-American actor (b. 1907)
- o Edward Arthur Thompson, British historian (b. 1914)
- January 2 – Pierre-Paul Schweitzer, French lawyer, former Managing Director of the IMF (b. 1912)
- January 3 – Frank Belknap Long, American writer (b. 1901)
- January 5
  - o Tip O'Neill, American Democratic politician, former speaker of the House of Representatives (b. 1912)
  - o Elmar Lipping, Estonian statesman and soldier (b. 1906)
  - o Brian Johnston, British cricket commentator (b. 1912)
- January 7 – Phoumi Vongvichit, Laotian politician, former president of the Republic (b. 1909)
- January 8 – Chandrashekarendra Saraswati, 68th Jagadguru in the Kanchi Kamakoti Peetam(b.1894)
- January 9
  - o Madge Ryan, Australian actress (b. 1919)
  - o Johnny Temple, American baseball player (b. 1927)
- January 11 – John Bradley, U.S. Navy flag raiser on Iwo Jima (b. 1923)
- January 12 – Samuel Bronston, American film producer and director (b. 1908)
- January 13 – Johan Jørgen Holst, Norwegian politician and diplomat (b. 1937)
- January 14
  - o Esther Ralston, American actress (b. 1902)
  - o Delio Rodríguez, Spanish cyclist (b. 1916)
  - o Zino Davidoff, Ukrainian tobacco entrepreneur (b. 1906)
  - o Federica Montseny, Spanish anarchist politician (b. 1905)
- January 15 – Harry Nilsson, American musician (b. 1941)
- January 16 – Frances Gifford, American actress (b. 1920)
- January 17
  - o Helen Stephens, American runner (b. 1918)
  - o Chung Il-kwon, South Korean politician and soldier, former Prime Minister (b. 1917)
- January 20
  - o Matt Busby, Scottish football manager (b. 1909)

- o Jaramogi Oginga Odinga, Kenyan politician (b. 1911)
- January 22
  - o Jean-Louis Barrault, French actor and director (b. 1910)
  - o Telly Savalas, American actor (b. 1922)
- January 23
  - o Brian Redhead, British journalist and broadcaster (b. 1929)
  - o Nikolai Ogarkov, Soviet marshal (b. 1917)
- January 25 – Stephen Cole Kleene, American mathematician (b. 1909)
- January 27 – Claude Akins, American actor (b. 1914)
- January 28 – Hal Smith, American character actor and voice-over artist (b. 1916)
- January 29
  - o Ulrike Maier, Austrian alpine skier (b. 1967)
  - o Nick Cravat, American actor and acrobat (b. 1912)
- January 30
  - o Bahjat Talhouni, Jordanian politician, former Prime Minister (b. 1913)
  - o Pierre Boulle, French author (b. 1912)

February

Joseph Cotten

Dinah Shore

Bill Hicks

- February 1 – Olan Soule, American character actor (b. 1909)
- February 2 – Marija Gimbutas, Lithuanian-American archeologist (b. 1921)
- February 3 – Walter Havighurst, American critic, novelist, literary and social historian (b. 1901)
- February 4 – Jane Arbor, British writer (b. 1903)
- February 6
  - Joseph Cotten, American actor (b. 1905)
  - Jack Kirby, American comic book writer and illustrator (b. 1917)
- February 7
  - Witold Lutosławski, Polish composer (b. 1913)
  - Arnold Smith, Canadian diplomat, the first Commonwealth Secretary-General (b. 1915)
- February 9 – Howard Martin Temin, American geneticist, recipient of the Nobel Prize in Physiology or Medicine (b. 1934)
- February 11
  - Neil Bonnett, American race car driver (b. 1946)
  - Sorrell Booke, American actor (b. 1930)
  - William Conrad, American actor (b. 1920)
  - Antonio Martín, Spanish cyclist (b. 1970)
- February 12 – Donald Judd, American artist (b. 1928)
- February 14
  - Christopher Lasch, American historian, moralist, and social critic (b. 1932)
  - Andrei Chikatilo, Russian serial killer (executed) (b. 1936)
- February 15 – the Maunula mummy, a Finnish man who lay dead in his apartment for six years until discovered

- February 17 – Randy Shilts, American author and activist (b. 1951)
- February 19 – Derek Jarman, English film director (b. 1942)
- February 22 – Papa John Creech, American fiddler (b. 1917)
- February 24
  - Jean Sablon, French singer (b. 1906)
  - Dinah Shore, American actress and singer (b. 1916)
  - Henry Milton Taylor, 3rd Governor-General of the Bahamas (b. 1903)
- February 25
  - Baruch Goldstein, American-born mass murder (b. 1956)
  - Jersey Joe Walcott, American boxer (b. 1914)
- February 26 – Bill Hicks, American comedian (b. 1961)
- February 28 – Josephat Karanja, Kenyan politician, former Vice President (b. 1931)

March

John Candy

Melina Mercouri

- March 2
  - Peter Cureton, Canadian actor and playwright

- o Anita Morris, American actress (b. 1943)
- March 4 – John Candy, Canadian comedian and actor (b. 1950)
- March 5 – Abdullah al-Sallal, North Yemeni soldier and statesmen, first president of the Yemen Arab Republic (b. 1917)
- March 6
  - o Ray Arcel, American boxing trainer (b. 1899)
  - o Melina Mercouri, Greek actress and politician (b. 1920)
- March 9
  - o Charles Bukowski, American writer (b. 1920)
  - o Fernando Rey, Spanish actor (b. 1917)
  - o Lawrence E. Spivak, American journalist (b. 1900)
- March 13 – Danny Barker, American jazz performer (b. 1909)
- March 17
  - o Ellsworth Vines, American tennis champion (b. 1911)
  - o Mai Zetterling, Swedish actor and director (b. 1925)
- March 20
  - o Lewis Grizzard, American writer and humorist (b. 1946)
- March 21
  - o Macdonald Carey, American actor (b. 1913)
  - o Dack Rambo, American actor (b. 1941)
- March 22 – Walter Lantz, American cartoonist (b. 1899)
- March 23
  - o Álvaro del Portillo, Spanish Roman Catholic bishop, prelate of Opus Dei (b. 1914)
  - o Luis Donaldo Colosio, Mexican politician, presidential candidate of the PRI party (assassinated) (b. 1950)
  - o Giulietta Masina, Italian actress (b. 1921)
- March 25 – Max Petitpierre, Member of the Swiss Federal Council (b. 1899)
- March 28
  - o Eugène Ionesco, Romanian-born playwright (b. 1909)
  - o Ira Murchison, American athlete (b. 1933)
- March 29 – Bill Travers, English actor and co-founder of the Born Free Foundation (b. 1922)

April

Kurt Cobain

Richard Nixon

- April 1
  - Léon Degrelle, Walloon Belgian Rexist and Nazi politician (b. 1906)
  - Robert Doisneau, French Photographer (b. 1912)
- April 2 – Betty Furness, American actress, author, and consumer advocate (b. 1916)
- April 3 – Jérôme Lejeune, French pediatrician and geneticist (b. 1926)
- April 5 – Kurt Cobain, American singer and songwriter (b. 1967)
- April 6
  - Juvénal Habyarimana, Rwandan banker and politician, 3rd President of Rwanda (assassinated) (b. 1937)
  - Cyprien Ntaryamira, Burundian politician, 5th President of Burundi (assassinated) (b. 1956)
- April 7
  - Agathe Uwilingiyimana, Prime Minister of Rwanda (assassinated) (b. 1953)
  - Albert Guðmundsson, Icelandic footballer and politician (b. 1923)

- o Golo Mann, German historian (b. 1909)
- April 10
  - o Sam B. Hall, American politician (b. 1924)
  - o Viktor Afanasyev, Soviet journalist (b. 1922)
- April 11 – Hal Lawrence, Canadian naval officer (b. 1920)
- April 14
  - o Manuel Andújar, Spanish writer (b. 1913)
  - o Hugh Springer, former Governor-General of Barbados (b. 1913)
- April 15 – John Curry, British figure skater (b. 1949)
- April 16 – Ralph Ellison, American writer (b. 1914)
- April 17 – Roger Wolcott Sperry, American neurobiologist, recipient of the Nobel Prize in Physiology or Medicine (b. 1913)
- April 22 – Richard Nixon, 37th President of the United States (b. 1913)
- April 24 – Masutatsu Ōyama, Korean-Japanese Karate master (b. 1923)
- April 27 – Lynne Frederick, English actress (b. 1954)
- April 28 – Berton Roueché, American writer (b. 1910)
- April 29
  - o Russell Kirk, American political philosopher (b. 1918)
  - o Sak Sutsakhan, Cambodian politician (b. 1928)
- April 30
  - o Roland Ratzenberger, Austrian Formula One driver (b. 1960)
  - o Richard Scarry, American author (b. 1919)
  - o Sorie Ibrahim Koroma, Former Prime Minister and Vice President of Sierra Leone (b. 1930)

May

Ayrton Senna

Jacqueline Kennedy Onassis

Erich Honecker

- May 1 – Ayrton Senna, Brazilian Formula One driver (b. 1960)
- May 2
  - William Albertini, English cricketer (b. 1913)
  - Dorothy Marie Donnelly, American poet (b. 1908)
- May 5 – Joe Layton, American director and choreographer (b. 1931)
- May 7 – Clement Greenberg, American art critic (b. 1909)
- May 8 – George Peppard, American actor (b. 1928)
- May 10 – John Wayne Gacy, American serial killer (b. 1942)
- May 12
  - Erik Erikson, Danish-American developmental psychologist (b. 1902)
  - John Smith, Scottish politician, leader of the British Labour Party (b. 1938)
  - Roy J. Plunkett, American chemist (b. 1910)
- May 14 – W. Graham Claytor, Jr., American railroad executive and 15th United States Secretary of the Navy (b. 1914)

- May 15
  - Royal Dano, American actor (b. 1922)
  - Gilbert Roland, Mexican-born actor (b. 1905)
- May 16 – Alain Cuny, French actor (b. 1908)
- May 17 – Étienne Hirsch, French engineer and administrator, former chairman of EURATOM (b. 1901)
- May 19
  - Jacqueline Kennedy Onassis, First Lady of the United States (b. 1929)
  - Henry Morgan, American comedian (b. 1915)
  - Luis Ocaña, Spanish bicycle racer (b. 1945)
- May 21
  - Giovanni Goria, Italian politician, former Prime Minister (b. 1943)
  - Masayoshi Ito, Japanese politician, former acting Prime Minister (b. 1913)
  - Ralph Miliband, Polish-born British academic (b. 1924)
  - Johan Hendrik Weidner, Belgian World War II resistance fighter (b. 1912)
- May 26 – Sonny Sharrock, American jazz musician (b. 1940)
- May 27 – Red Rodney, American trumpeter (b. 1927)
- May 29 – Erich Honecker, former Communist leader of the East Germany (b. 1912)
- May 30
  - Juan Carlos Onetti, Uruguayan novelist (b. 1909)
  - Marcel Bich, French manufacturer and co-founder of Bic (b. 1914)
  - Ezra Taft Benson, American religious leader, thirteenth president of The Church of Jesus Christ of Latter-day Saints (LDS Church) (b. 1899)

June

- June 2 – David Stove, Australian philosopher (suicide) (b. 1927)
- June 3 – Jack Cowie, New Zealand cricketer (b. 1912)
- June 4
  - Benedict J. Semmes, Jr., American admiral (b. 1913)

- o Peter Thorneycroft, British Conservative politician (b. 1909)
- o Massimo Troisi, Italian actor (b. 1953)
- June 6 – Barry Sullivan, American actor (b. 1912)
- June 7 – Dennis Potter, English dramatist (b. 1935)
- June 9 – Jan Tinbergen, Dutch economist, Nobel Prize laureate (b. 1903)
- June 10 – Edward Kienholz, American installation artist and sculptor (b. 1927)
- June 12
  - o Menachem Mendel Schneerson, the Lubavitcher Rebbe (b. 1902)
  - o Nicole Brown Simpson, former wife of O. J. Simpson (b. 1959)
  - o Chris Latta, American voice actor & comedian (b. 1949)
- June 13 – K. T. Stevens, American actress (b. 1919)
- June 14 – Henry Mancini, American composer and arranger (b. 1924)
- June 15
  - o Kristen Pfaff, American bassist (b. 1967)
  - o Manos Hatzidakis, Greek composer (b. 1925)
- June 20 – Jay Miner, American computer pioneer (b. 1932)
- June 21 – William Wilson Morgan, American astronomer and astrophysicist (b. 1906)
- June 29 – Kurt Eichhorn, German conductor (b. 1908)

July

Dick Sargent

Kim Il-sung

- July 2
  - Roberto Balado, Cuban boxer, 1992 Gold medalist (b. 1969)
  - Maung Maung, former President of Myanmar (b. 1925)
- July 3 – Lew Hoad, Australian tennis champion (b. 1934)
- July 6 – Ahmet Haxhiu, Albanian political activist (b. 1932)
- July 7
  - Friedrich August Freiherr von der Heydte, German Luftwaffe Officer (b. 1907)
  - Cameron Mitchell, American actor (b. 1918)
  - Anita Garvin. American Actress (b. 1907), Famous (Laurel & Hardy) Co-star
- July 8
  - Dick Sargent, American actor (b. 1930)
  - Kim Il-sung, President of North Korea (b. 1912)
  - Christian-Jaque, French film director (b. 1904)
- July 11 – Gary Kildall, American computer inventor (b. 1942)
- July 14 – César Tovar, Venezuelan baseball player (Minnesota Twins) (b. 1940)
- July 16
  - Patricio Carvajal, Chilean admiral, minister and diplomat (b. 1916)
  - Julian Schwinger, American physicist, recipient of the Nobel Prize in Physics (b. 1918)
- July 17 – Jean Borotra, French tennis champion (b. 1898)
- July 19 – Ray Flaherty, American football coach (Washington Redskins) and member of the Pro Football Hall of Fame (b. 1903)
- July 20 – Paul Delvaux, Belgian painter (b. 1897)

- July 21
  - Marijac, French cartoonist
  - Pere Calders, Spanish writer and cartoonist (b. 1912)
- July 22 – Alexandre Hogue, American painter (b. 1898)
- July 23 – Lennox Sebe, President of Ciskei bantustan (b. 1926)
- July 29 – Dorothy Hodgkin, British chemist, Nobel Prize laureate (b. 1910)

August

- August 4 – Giovanni Spadolini, Italian politician, former Prime Minister (b. 1925)
- August 6 – Domenico Modugno, Italian singer, songwriter, actor and politician (b. 1928)
- August 7
  - Larry Martyn, comedy actor (b. 1934)
  - Rosa Chacel, Spanish writer (b. 1898)
- August 11 – Peter Cushing, English actor (b. 1913)
- August 13 – Manfred Wörner, German politician and diplomat, General Secretary of NATO (b. 1934)
- August 14 – Elias Canetti, Bulgarian-born writer, Nobel Prize laureate (b. 1905)
- August 17 – Jack Sharkey, American boxer (b. 1902)
- August 18 – Richard Laurence Millington Synge, English chemist, Nobel Prize laureate (b. 1914)
- August 19 – Linus Pauling, American chemist, recipient of the Nobel Prize in Chemistry and Peace (b. 1901)
- August 21
  - Anita Lizana, Chilean tennis champion (b. 1915)
  - Michael Peters, American choreographer (b. 1948)
- August 23 – Zoltán Fábri, Hungarian film director (b. 1917)
- August 28 – David Wright, South African poet (b. 1920)
- August 30 – Lindsay Anderson, British film director (b. 1923)

September

Karl Popper

Robert Bloch

Louis Ferdinand, Prince of Prussia

- September 2 – Roy Castle, British entertainer (b. 1932)
- September 5 – Shimshon Amitsur, Israeli mathematician and Israel Prize recipient (b. 1921)
- September 6
  - Nicky Hopkins, British musician (b. 1944)
  - Duccio Tessari, Italian director and screenwriter (b. 1926)
  - Paul Xuereb, Maltese politician, former acting President (b. 1923)

- September 7
  - James Clavell, British writer (b. 1921)
  - Dennis Morgan, American actor and singer (b. 1908)
  - Terence Young, British film director (b. 1915)
- September 8 – János Szentágothai, Hungarian anatomist (b. 1912)
- September 9 – Patrick O'Neal, American actor (b. 1927)
- September 11 – Jessica Tandy, English actress (b. 1909)
- September 12
  - Tom Ewell, American actor (b. 1909)
  - Boris Yegorov, Russian cosmonaut (b. 1937)
- September 15
  - Moana Pozzi, Italian porn actress (b. 1961)
  - Mark Stevens, American actor (b. 1916)
- September 16 – Jack Dodson, American actor (b. 1931)
- September 17
  - Vitas Gerulaitis, American tennis champion (b. 1954)
  - Karl Popper, Austrian and British philosopher (b. 1902)
- September 18 – Franco Moschino, Italian fashion designer (b. 1950)
- September 19
  - Alberto Closas, Spanish actor (b. 1921)
  - Joseph Iléo, Congolese politician, former Prime Minister of the Democratic Republic of the Congo (b. 1921)
- September 20
  - Abioseh Nicol, Sierra Leonean diplomat, UN official and author (b. 1924)
  - Jule Styne, British-born songwriter (b. 1905)
- September 22 – Bud Sagendorf, American cartoonist (b. 1915)
- September 23 – Robert Bloch, American writer (b. 1917)
- September 24 – Sir David Napley, British solicitor (b. 1915)
- September 26 – Louis Ferdinand, Prince of Prussia (b. 1907)
- September 27 – Carlos Lleras Restrepo, former president of Colombia (b. 1908)
- September 28 – José Francisco Ruiz Massieu, Mexican politician, general secretary of the PRI party (assassinated) (b. 1946)
- September 30

- André Michel Lwoff, French microbiologist, recipient of the Nobel Prize in Physiology or Medicine (b. 1902)
- Roberto Eduardo Viola, former military president of Argentina (b. 1924)

October

Burt Lancaster

Raúl Juliá

- October 2 – Harriet Nelson, American actress (b. 1909)
- October 3
  - Tim Asch, Anthropologist, photographer and ethnographic filmmaker (b. 1932)
  - Dub Taylor, American actor (b. 1907)
- October 4 – Danny Gatton, American guitarist (b. 1945)
- October 7
  - Niels Kaj Jerne, English immunologist, recipient of the Nobel Prize in Physiology or Medicine (b. 1911)
  - James Hill), British film and TV director (b. 1919)
- October 15 – Sarah Kofman, French philosopher (b. 1934)
- October 19 – Martha Raye, American actress (b. 1916)
- October 18 – Conchita Montes, Spanish actress (b. 1914)
- October 19 – Oldřich Černík, former Prime Minister of Czechoslovakia (b. 1921)

- October 20
  - Sergei Bondarchuk, Russian film director (b. 1920)
  - Burt Lancaster, American actor (b. 1913)
- October 21 – Benoît Régent, French actor (b. 1953)
- October 22 – Fabio Grobart, Cuban Communist politician (b. 1905)
- October 23 – Robert Lansing, American actor (b. 1928)
- October 24
  - Raúl Juliá, Puerto Rican actor (b. 1940)
  - Gamini Dissanayake, Sri Lankan opposition leader and presidential candidate (assassinated) (b. 1942)
- October 25 – Mildred Natwick, American actress (b. 1905)
- October 28 – Calvin S. Fuller, American physical chemist (b. 1902)
- October 29 – Shlomo Goren, Israeli Chief Rabbi (b. 1918)

November

Cab Calloway

Jeffrey Dahmer

- November 1 – Noah Beery, Jr., American actor (b. 1913)

- November 4 – Fred "Sonic" Smith, American guitarist (b. 1949)
- November 5 – Johan Heyns, Afrikaner theologian and critic of Apartheid (b. 1928)
- November 9 – Priscilla Morrill, American actress (b. 1927)
- November 10 – Carmen McRae, American jazz singer (b. 1920)
- November 11 – Pedro Zamora, Cuban-born AIDS activist (b. 1972)
- November 12 – Wilma Rudolph, American athlete (b. 1940)
- November 12 – J. I. M. Stewart, Scottish novelist (b. 1906)
- November 13 – Motoo Kimura, Japanese geneticist (b. 1924)
- November 14 – Tom Villard, American actor (b. 1953)
- November 16
  - Doris Speed, English actress (b. 1899)
  - Dino Valente, American musician (b. 1937)
- November 18
  - Cab Calloway, American jazz singer and bandleader (b. 1908)
  - Peter Ledger, Australian artist (b. 1945)
- November 20 – John Lucarotti, British-born television writer (b. 1926)
- November 22 – Charles Upham, New Zealand soldier, double Victoria Cross winner (b. 1908)
- November 23 – Art Barr, American professional wrestler (b. 1966)
- November 28
  - Jeffrey Dahmer, American serial killer (b. 1960)
  - Buster Edwards, English Great train robber (b. 1932)
- November 30
  - Guy Debord, French Marxist theorist, writer, filmmaker (b. 1931)
  - Lionel Stander, American actor (b. 1908)

December

Dean Rusk

- December 6 – Gian Maria Volontè, Italian actor (b. 1933)
- December 8 – Antônio Carlos Jobim, Brazilian composer (b. 1927)
- December 10 – Alex Wilson, Canadian and Notre Dame athlete (b. 1905)
- December 11
    - Philip Phillips, American archaeologist (b. 1900)
    - Carl Marzani, American political documentary filmmaker, author, editor and publisher (b. 1912)
- December 12
    - Donna J. Stone, American poet and philanthropist (b. 1933)
    - Stuart Roosa, American astronaut (b. 1933)
- December 13 – Hu Lanqi, Chinese woman revolutionary, general, and writer (b. 1901)
- December 18 – Lilia Skala, Austrian-born actress (b. 1896)
- December 20
    - Hans Herlin, German novelist (b. 1925)
    - Dean Rusk, 54th United States Secretary of State (b. 1909)
- December 23 – Sebastian Shaw, English actor (b. 1905)
- December 24
    - John Boswell, American historian (b. 1947)
    - Rossano Brazzi, Italian actor (b. 1916)
    - John Osborne, English playwright (b. 1929)
- December 25 – Zail Singh, Indian politician and 7th President of India (b. 1916)
- December 27

- Fanny Cradock, British television chef and restaurant critic (b. 1909)
- Peter May, English cricketer (b. 1929)
- J. B. L. Reyes, Filipino jurist (b. 1902)

Nobel Prizes

- Physics – Bertram N. Brockhouse, Clifford Glenwood Shull
- Chemistry – George Andrew Olah
- Medicine – Alfred G. Gilman, Martin Rodbell
- Literature – Kenzaburō Ōe
- Peace – Yasser Arafat, Shimon Peres, Yitzhak Rabin
- Nobel Memorial Prize in Economic Sciences – Reinhard Selten, John Forbes Nash, John Harsanyi

In the News

Tonya Harding wins the national Figure Skating championship title but is stripped of her title following an attack on her rival Nancy Kerrigan.

Channel Tunnel opened on May 6th between England and France.

Brazil Wins 1994 World Cup in United States.

Netscape Navigator released quickly becoming market leader for browsing the web.

OJ Simpson flees police in his white ford bronco.

The New UK Lottery Introduced with an estimated jackpot of £7m.

Ayrton Senna of Brazil, age 34, is tragically killed during the San Marino Grand Prix in Imola, Italy.

Lisa Marie Presley marries Michael Jackson.

Popular Films - The Shawshank Redemption, Forrest Gump, The Lion King, True Lies.

New Sunday Trading Laws allows shops in Britain to open legally on Sundays.

Sweden and Norway vote on whether or not to join the European Union.

1994 Calendar

January 1994

Sun	Mon	Tue	Wed	Thu	Fri	Sat
						1
2	3	4	5	6	7	8
9	10	11	12	13	14	15
16	17	18	19	20	21	22
23	24	25	26	27	28	29
30	31					

February 1994

Sun	Mon	Tue	Wed	Thu	Fri	Sat
		1	2	3	4	5
6	7	8	9	10	11	12
13	14	15	16	17	18	19
20	21	22	23	24	25	26
27	28					

March 1994

Sun	Mon	Tue	Wed	Thu	Fri	Sat
		1	2	3	4	5
6	7	8	9	10	11	12
13	14	15	16	17	18	19
20	21	22	23	24	25	26
27	28	29	30	31		

April 1994

Sun	Mon	Tue	Wed	Thu	Fri	Sat
					1	2
3	4	5	6	7	8	9
10	11	12	13	14	15	16
17	18	19	20	21	22	23
24	25	26	27	28	29	30

May 1994

Sun	Mon	Tue	Wed	Thu	Fri	Sat
1	2	3	4	5	6	7
8	9	10	11	12	13	14
15	16	17	18	19	20	21
22	23	24	25	26	27	28
29	30	31				

June 1994

Sun	Mon	Tue	Wed	Thu	Fri	Sat
			1	2	3	4
5	6	7	8	9	10	11
12	13	14	15	16	17	18
19	20	21	22	23	24	25
26	27	28	29	30		

July 1994

Sun	Mon	Tue	Wed	Thu	Fri	Sat
					1	2
3	4	5	6	7	8	9
10	11	12	13	14	15	16
17	18	19	20	21	22	23
24	25	26	27	28	29	30
31						

August 1994

Sun	Mon	Tue	Wed	Thu	Fri	Sat
	1	2	3	4	5	6
7	8	9	10	11	12	13
14	15	16	17	18	19	20
21	22	23	24	25	26	27
28	29	30	31			

September 1994

Sun	Mon	Tue	Wed	Thu	Fri	Sat
				1	2	3
4	5	6	7	8	9	10
11	12	13	14	15	16	17
18	19	20	21	22	23	24
25	26	27	28	29	30	

October 1994

Sun	Mon	Tue	Wed	Thu	Fri	Sat
						1
2	3	4	5	6	7	8
9	10	11	12	13	14	15
16	17	18	19	20	21	22
23	24	25	26	27	28	29
30	31					

November 1994

Sun	Mon	Tue	Wed	Thu	Fri	Sat
		1	2	3	4	5
6	7	8	9	10	11	12
13	14	15	16	17	18	19
20	21	22	23	24	25	26
27	28	29	30			

December 1994

Sun	Mon	Tue	Wed	Thu	Fri	Sat
				1	2	3
4	5	6	7	8	9	10
11	12	13	14	15	16	17
18	19	20	21	22	23	24
25	26	27	28	29	30	31